BABE RUTH

SUPER SLUGGER

JOE LEVIT

LERNER PUBLICATIONS ◆ MINNEAPOLIS

To Huy Huynh, a loyal friend and also a heavy hitter

Lerner Publications Company
An imprint of Lerner Publishing Group, Inc.
241 First Avenue North
Minneapolis, MN 55401 USA

For reading levels and more information, look up this title at www.lernerbooks.com.

Main body text set in Myriad Pro Semibold.
Typeface provided by Adobe.

Editor: Shee Yang **Designer:** Susan Fienhage
Lerner team: Martha Kranes

Library of Congress Cataloging-in-Publication Data

Names: Levit, Joseph, author. | Lerner Publications Company.
Title: Babe Ruth : super slugger / Joe Levit.
Description: Minneapolis : Lerner Publications, 2021. | Series: Epic Sports Bios (Lerner Sports) | Includes bibliographical references and index. | Audience: Ages 7–11 years | Audience: Grades 2–3 | Summary: "From the Boston Red Sox to the New York Yankees, Babe Ruth's epic rise to the Baseball Hall of Fame is one to remember. Learn more about Ruth in this epic biography"—Provided by publisher.
Identifiers: LCCN 2019052556 (print) | LCCN 2019052557 (ebook) | ISBN 9781541597471 (Library Binding) | ISBN 9781728413396 (Paperback) | ISBN 9781728400082 (eBook)
Subjects: LCSH: Ruth, Babe, 1895--1948—Juvenile literature. | Baseball players—United States—Biography—Juvenile literature. | Boston Red Sox (Baseball team)—History. | Pitchers (Baseball)—Biography—Juvenile literature. | New York Yankees (Baseball team)—History. | Outfielders (Baseball)—Biography—Juvenile literature. | National Baseball Hall of Fame and Museum—History. | Baseball—United States—History.
Classification: LCC GV865.R8 L48 2021 (print) | LCC GV865.R8 (ebook) | DDC 796.357092 [B]—dc23

LC record available at https://lccn.loc.gov/2019052556
LC ebook record available at https://lccn.loc.gov/2019052557

Manufactured in the United States of America
1-47851-48291-3/18/2020

CONTENTS

THE START OF SOMETHING SPECIAL

In 1913, Mount St. Joseph's athletic director Brother Gilbert drove to St. Mary's Industrial School for Boys in Baltimore, Maryland. Brother Gilbert was there to observe an 18-year-old baseball player named George Herman Ruth Jr.

Babe Ruth (*right*) began playing baseball when he arrived at St. Mary's in 1902.

FACTS AT A GLANCE

Date of birth: February 6, 1895

Position: right field

League: Major League Baseball (MLB)

Professional highlights: earned a pro contract as a 19-year-old; went 13–7 as a pitcher in the 1918 season; hit over .300 as a batter in 1918; was part of eight World Series–winning teams; inducted into the Hall of Fame in 1936

Personal highlights: developed his baseball skills at St. Mary's Industrial School for Boys; made it to MLB with the Boston Red Sox; played an important role in the legacy of the New York Yankees

One of Brother Gilbert's own players had told him that Ruth was the best hitter he'd ever seen. Ruth stepped to the plate. The pitcher motioned for his team to move farther back. The right fielder moved so far back, he was standing in the outfield of another baseball game. The game on the other field paused their play. Everyone wanted to watch Ruth.

On the first pitch of his at-bat, Ruth crushed the ball, landing it in the other field. For Brother Gilbert, it was a glimpse into the future. Ruth would crush balls over outfielders' heads for years to come.

Ruth spent 12 years at St. Mary's Industrial School for Boys.

THE MEAN STREETS

George Herman Ruth Jr. was born in Baltimore on February 6, 1895. His parents struggled to earn enough money to support the family. As a kid, George often skipped school, teased police officers, and got

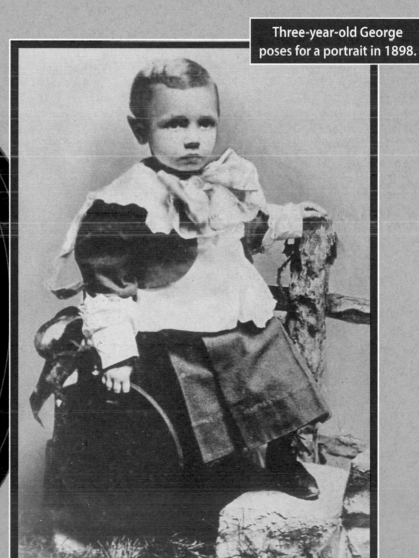

Three-year-old George poses for a portrait in 1898.

A STITCH IN TIME

St. Mary's offered classes such as gardening, tailoring, baking, shoemaking, and carpentry. George became good at making shirts by training in a tailor shop located in the school's laundry building. But it was his talent for baseball that set him up for life.

into fistfights. When George was seven, his parents sent him to St. Mary's, a nearby Catholic school. The school was for boys who were homeless or considered too troublesome to manage in other schools.

St. Mary's would become George's home for the rest of his childhood. The school intended to teach all students a trade that could help them get by as adults.

Brother Matthias Boutilier was St. Mary's athletic director. He stood 6 feet 6 (2 m) tall and weighed 250 pounds (113 kg). He introduced George to baseball and would stand by him for the rest of Matthias's life. Brother Matthias was a talented baseball player. He would toss a ball into the air with his left hand and swing the bat with his right. He could whack a ball hard enough to clear the fence in center field 350 feet (107 m) away.

Brother Matthias's skill made a big impression on George. "I would just stand there and watch him, bug-eyed,"

George (*left*) as a young teen on St. Mary's baseball team

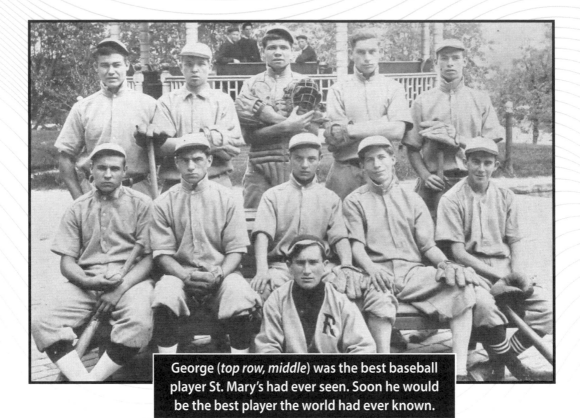

George (*top row, middle*) was the best baseball player St. Mary's had ever seen. Soon he would be the best player the world had ever known.

George said. "I had never seen anything like that in my life, nor anyone who was even close to Brother Matthias when it came to manliness, kindness, and grace." George copied Brother Matthais's swing and practiced often. Soon George was playing on teams with boys three to four years older than he was.

GETTING NOTICED

When he was 15, George teased a pitcher on St. Mary's team. Brother Matthias challenged George to get up on the pitcher's mound if he thought it was so easy. Soon George was performing at a high level at the plate and on the mound.

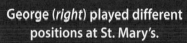
George (*right*) played different positions at St. Mary's.

Jack Dunn (*middle*) and Ruth (*left*)
continued their friendship until
Dunn's death in 1928.

After seeing Ruth play in 1913, Brother Gilbert asked
Baltimore Orioles owner Jack Dunn to watch Ruth play
baseball. At the time, the Orioles were a minor-league team.
Dunn liked what he saw and offered Ruth $600 to play a
six-month season with his team. As Ruth left St. Mary's,
Brother Matthias told him, "You'll make it, George."

BORN A PITCHER

Right away, Ruth felt at home as a pitcher. "As soon as I got out there I felt a strange relationship with the pitcher's mound," he said. "It was as if I'd been born out there. Pitching just felt like the most natural thing in the world. Striking out batters was easy."

As the newest player on the Orioles, Ruth's teammates started calling him Babe as a joke. But soon enough, everyone was calling him Babe. In June, Dunn gave Ruth a raise. Ruth would receive $1,800 a month for the next six months.

THE BOSTON YEARS

In July 1914, Dunn sold some of his players to avoid bankruptcy. The Red Sox, a major-league team, welcomed Ruth to Boston. Off the field, Ruth began dating his future wife, Helen Woodford. On the field, he had his moments, but Ruth's overall performance was not up

Ruth struggled to adjust to the fast pace of the major leagues.

to MLB standards. Soon he was sitting on the bench, and eventually the Red Sox sent him back to the minors.

Discouraged and sad, Ruth received a letter from Brother Matthias. "You're doing fine, George. I'm proud of you," the letter said. Later that season, Ruth led his minor-league team to a championship. Impressed, the Red Sox brought him back up to the big leagues.

Woodford and Ruth met in July of 1914. They were married three months later at St. Paul Catholic Church in Ellicott City, Maryland.

Ruth throws a pitch for the Red Sox.

    After the season, Ruth and Woodford married. In 1915, he won 18 games as a pitcher and hit a towering home run against the Yankees. At only 20 years old, Ruth was the second-best hitter on the team. The Red Sox took the pennant and advanced to the World Series against the Philadelphia Phillies. Boston won the series 4–1.

During the 1916 season, Ruth won 23 games as a pitcher. The Red Sox took the pennant and faced the Brooklyn Dodgers in the World Series, winning in five games.

The 1917 season was a bust. World War I (1914–1918) had been raging for the past few years. Many players left baseball to fight and spirits were low for the players that remained. Ruth began getting into fights on the field. He won 24 games as a pitcher that year, but the Red Sox ended their season in third place.

From left: Ruth with his Red Sox teammates Ernie Shore, Rube Foster, and Del Gainer

Ruth returned in 1918 determined and focused. He went 13–7 as a pitcher. He hit over .300 as a batter. But he knew that the workload on the mound and at the plate would catch up to him someday. "I can do it this season all right, and not feel it, for I am young and strong and don't mind the work," he said. "But I wouldn't guarantee to do it for many seasons." The Red Sox reached the World Series once again. Ruth pitched and won two games. The team beat the Chicago Cubs four games to two.

A MASTER ON THE MOUND

During the 1918 World Series, Ruth set a record that would stand for 42 years. He pitched 29 scoreless innings of play. Ruth later claimed he was prouder of that mark than all of his records as a hitter. "He would have been a Hall of Fame pitcher had he never hit a home run," said *New York Times* sportswriter Dave Anderson.

Ruth giving Miller Huggins, the manager of the New York Yankees, a tour of Riverside Drive in Manhattan in 1923

Ruth had become a big celebrity. He had fans all over the world and lived life in luxury. He often bought himself and others expensive gifts. Still, Ruth never forgot his tough childhood. He regularly visited St. Mary's and schools like it, giving away gifts and signing autographs for children. For Brother Matthias, Ruth gave him two cars.

In the 1919 season, Ruth decided to stop pitching. He also wanted $15,000 a year on a two-year contract. Red Sox owner Harry Frazee and Ruth agreed to a three-year deal worth $10,000 per season.

In an exhibition game, Ruth blasted a 579-foot (176 m) home run. It was the longest hit ever at the time. Ruth hit 29 home runs that year, a new major-league record. Four of the homers were grand slams. That was another record, one that wouldn't be broken for 40 years.

Ruth with his arms outstretched in the locker room after hitting three home runs in a single day

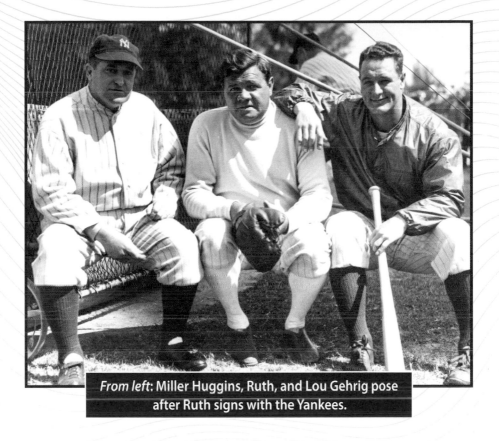

From left: Miller Huggins, Ruth, and Lou Gehrig pose after Ruth signs with the Yankees.

After the season, Frazee needed money to pay off debts. He sold Ruth to the New York Yankees for $100,000 in cash and a loan of $300,000. The Red Sox finished dead last in the standings in nine of the next 11 seasons. Meanwhile, the Yankees had the best hitter in the big leagues.

A STAR IN NEW YORK

Ruth needed time to adjust to his new team. He failed to hit home runs in exhibition games and stayed out late every night. A reporter once asked his baseball roommate what Ruth was like. "I don't room with him, I room with his suitcase," the roommate said.

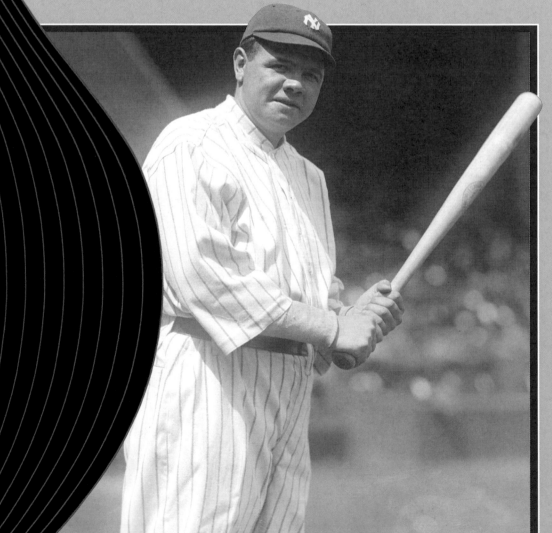

Ruth and Woodford were together for 11 years.

By the time Ruth and Woodford officially separated in 1925, they had a three-year-old daughter named Dorothy. Ruth began seeing Claire Merritt Hodgson, a widow with a daughter named Julia. Then, in January 1929, Woodford died tragically in a house fire. In April, Ruth and Hodgson married. Ruth adopted Julia, and Hodgson

Ruth and Hodgson at the opening of the 1929 American League season at Yankee Stadium.

adopted Dorothy. The family would stay together for the rest of Ruth's life.

By his second season with the Yankees, Ruth was on fire. His skill pushed the team to new heights. He hit .380 with 59 home runs that year. The team clinched the pennant but lost the World Series to the Giants 5–3. The Yankees would face the Giants again in the 1922 World Series. This time, New York lost in a 4–0 sweep.

Yankee Stadium opened in 1923. Fans knew the stadium as the House That Ruth Built—and it lived up to the name. Ruth hit .393 that year and helped defeat the Giants in the World Series. Ruth was already a big star, but his performance in the World Series confirmed that he was a living baseball legend.

Ruth (*right*) slides into third base during the 1923 World Series.

In 1926, Ruth hit 47 homers and won the league's Most Valuable Player Award. The Yankees made it to the World Series yet again, but the St. Louis Cardinals claimed victory 4–3.

The following season, Ruth banged out a record 60 homers. The Yankees were unstoppable. They swept the Pittsburgh Pirates in the World Series. In 1928, they dominated the Cardinals in the World Series 4–0. Four years

Ruth's super slugging led the Yankees to four World Series championships.

Ruth's final appearance at Yankee Stadium on June 13, 1948

later, Ruth helped the Yankees take the World Series one last time against the Chicago Cubs in a four-game sweep.

Ruth played his last major-league game in 1935 after being sold to the Boston Braves. He was 40 years old and knew his pro baseball days were over. Babe was inducted into the National Baseball Hall of Fame the following year. He spent retirement quietly with his wife and children, only making public appearances when necessary. Ruth died on August 16, 1948. He was 53 years old.

SIGNIFICANT STATS

Career home runs: 714
Third behind Barry Bonds (762) and Hank Aaron (755)

Career runs batted in: 2,214
Second behind Hank Aaron (2,297)

Career earned run average as a pitcher: 2.28

Led MLB in home runs: **12 times**

Led MLB in runs scored: **8 times**

Won the World Series: **7 times**

GLOSSARY

at-bat: a batter's appearance at the plate to face the pitcher

bankruptcy: a legal process for seeking relief from debts if unable to pay money owed

exhibition game: a game that does not count towards the final standings or the league championship

grand slam: a home run hit when each base is occupied by a base runner

inducted: formally admitted someone to an organization based on achievements

minor league: a pro baseball league where players train to join the major leagues

pennant: the championship of MLB's American League or National League. Pennant winners play in the World Series.

plate: the five-sided base where a batter stands

World Series: the championship series of MLB

9   Willborn Hampton, *Up Close: Babe Ruth* (New York: Viking Books, 2009), 38.

10   Hampton, 48.

12   Hampton, 48.

13   "Babe Ruth Biography," Biography Online, last modified February 8, 2018, https://www.biographyonline.net/sport/babe-ruth-biography.html.

15   Hampton, *Babe Ruth*, 76.

18   Brian Martin, *The Man Who Made Babe Ruth: Brother Matthias of St. Mary's School* (Jefferson, NC: McFarland, 2020), 79.

18   "SportsCentury: Babe Ruth," YouTube video, 43:10, posted by Max Carey, April 21, 2018, 12:40, https://www.youtube.com/watch?v=5GkZRw21kho.

22   Frank Ceresi, "Artifacts from the Greatest Baseball Player of All Time," Baseball Almanac, accessed March 16, 2020), https://www.baseball-almanac.com/treasure/autont003.shtml.

FURTHER INFORMATION

Babe Ruth Facts for Kids
https://kids.kiddle.co/Babe_Ruth

Babe Ruth Stats
https://www.baseball-reference.com/players/r/ruthba01.shtml

Bechtel, Mark. Sports Illustrated Kids *Big Book of Who: Baseball*. New York: Liberty Street, 2017.

Fishman, Jon M. *Baseball's G.O.A.T.: Babe Ruth, Mike Trout, and More*. Minneapolis: Lerner Publications, 2020.

Jacobs, Greg. *The Everything Kids' Baseball Book: From Baseball's History to Today's Favorite Players—with Lots of Home Run Fun in Between!* Avon, MA: Adams Media, 2018.

Major League Baseball
https://www.mlb.com

INDEX

PHOTO ACKNOWLEDGMENTS

Image credits: The History Collection/Alamy Stock Photo, pp. 4, 9; Andrey_Popov/Shutterstock.com, pp. 5, 28; History and Art Collection/Alamy Stock Photo, pp. 6, 10; Mark Rucker/Transcendental Graphics/Getty Images, p. 7; Mark Rucker/Transcendental Graphics/Getty Images, pp. 11, 19; Buyenlarge/Getty Images, p. 12; Library of Congress (LC-DIG-npcc-00316), p. 14; Keystone/FPG/Getty Images, p. 15; Francis P. Burke Collection/Wikimedia Commons (Public Domain), p. 16; GL Archive/Alamy Stock Photo, p. 17; Library of Congress, p. 20; Sports Studio Photos/Getty Images, p. 21; Bettmann Archive/Getty Images, pp. 22, 23, 24, 25, 26; Sporting News/Getty Images, p. 27.

Cover: 1920 MLB Photos/Getty Images; Conde Nast Collection Editorial/Getty Images.